The Great Proclamation

Proclamation

A BOOK FOR YOUNG AMERICANS

The Great Proclamation

★ ★ A BOOK FOR YOUNG AMERICANS ★ ★

by

HENRY STEELE COMMAGER

THE **BOBBS-MERRILL** COMPANY, INC.
A SUBSIDIARY OF HOWARD W. SAMS & CO., INC.
Publishers · INDIANAPOLIS · NEW YORK

Contents

List of Illustrations

The *Great*

Proclamation

A BOOK FOR YOUNG AMERICANS

I

IN NOVEMBER 1860, Abraham Lincoln of Illinois was elected President of the United States. The next February, on his way to Washington to take office, he stopped off at Philadelphia to make a short speech. He spoke at the old Independence Hall, where the Fathers of the Revolution had debated the Declaration of Independence. Naturally enough, Lincoln talked about the Great Declaration.

What did it mean? It meant, said Lincoln, that

> in due time the weights should be lifted from the shoulders of all men . . . that *all* should have an equal chance.

11

Advertisement announcing arrival of slaves.

Notice that Lincoln said *all* men, not just all white men, and not just all Americans, for that matter. South of the Potomac River—you could see across it from the top of the White House or from the newly built Washington Monument—and south of the Ohio River, there were four million men and women and children who were not free, but slaves. All of them were Negroes.

They had been carrying weights all their lives, and the weights were sometimes very heavy. Did Lincoln mean that the weights should be lifted from their shoulders, too? They did not have an equal chance— or any kind of chance at all—except with the permission of their masters. Did Lincoln mean that *they* should have an equal chance?

Slaves pass by the Capitol.

A slave auction in Virginia.

Yes, he did.

"I have always disliked slavery," he said. "If slavery is not wrong, nothing is wrong." And, again, "No man is good enough to govern another man without that man's consent." In reply to someone who was defending slavery, he said, "Whenever I hear anyone arguing for slavery, I feel a strong impulse to see it tried on him personally."

Lincoln's words were: "I have always disliked slavery." There was nothing special about that. Millions of people disliked slavery, and not all of them in the North, either. There were many Southerners, like rich, aristocratic Mrs. Chesnut of Charleston, in

14

South Carolina, who could say, "I hate slavery."

But among all those millions who disliked slavery, Lincoln, and Lincoln alone, was able to do something about it. He was able to free the slaves.

Imagine being able to set four million people free!

He had not planned it that way—not in the beginning, anyway. "If all earthly power were given me," he had said, "I should not know what to do." He had always disliked slavery, always thought it wrong, always fought it when he could. That did not amount to much.

It was like saying, as all of us do now, that we dislike war. Everybody dislikes war. But we go right on preparing for it, and even fighting wars when necessary. It is not always easy to put an end to things that we know are wrong. Life is not so simple.

Abraham Lincoln had known that from the beginning.

After all, Lincoln grew up with slavery. He was born a Southerner—down in Kentucky. He married a Southerner—a girl from Kentucky. Even after his father had moved the family across the Ohio River into Indiana, and after young Abraham himself had moved on to the new state of Illinois, he was still surrounded by Southerners. Almost everyone who settled in that part of Indiana and Illinois came from the South.

Many of the Southerners Lincoln knew owned slaves.

The Lincoln House in Springfield, Illinois.

That did not mean these people were wicked.
Lincoln knew that they were just as good as he was;
he was never one for calling people wicked, anyway.
He knew that they were caught in a system that they
had not made, a system they could not unmake.
There it was, and they had to make the best of it.

Many of the Southerners tried hard to take the
curse off slavery. They were kind to their slaves.
They gave them plenty to eat and drink, and fire-

16

wood and blankets for the cold nights. They took
care of their slaves when they were sick or when
they were old.

The trouble was not so much with the slave-
owners. It was with slavery itself. Slavery was, as
the poet Stephen Vincent Benét wrote later,

> an unjust thing
> That some tamed into mercy, being wise,
> But could not starve the tiger from its eyes,
> Or make it feed where beasts of mercy feed.

Way back in 1837, before he was thirty years old,
Lincoln had stood up to be counted against slavery.

Negro child before fireplace.

It was when he was in the State Legislature of Illinois. He was a rustic figure—tall, gangling, awkward, all bones and smiles and wit—and as yet a mere nobody. The Legislature had passed a resolution saying that slavery was sacred. That is the very word they used! They said people were to leave it alone, and be quiet.

The word "sacred" was more than Lincoln could swallow. He drew up a resolution saying that "the institution of slavery is founded on . . . injustice." He was able to get only one other man to vote for this, but it did not matter. He already knew what James Russell Lowell later put into verse—that

> They are slaves who dare not be
> In the right with two or three.

A few years later, Lincoln and his friend Joshua Speed took a trip on a steamboat. They went down the Ohio and Mississippi rivers to New Orleans, a thousand miles to the south. It was almost like taking a trip to the moon today. This was not his first voyage, but it was the one that made the strongest impression on him. Years later, he wrote Speed about it:

. . . In 1841, you and I had together a tedious low-water trip. . . . You may remember, as I well do, that from Louisville to the mouth of the Ohio there were, on board, ten or a dozen slaves, shackled together with irons. That sight

Lincoln watching a New Orleans slave auction.

was a continual torment to me, and I see something like it every time I touch the Ohio or any
other slave border.

But Lincoln was, above all, a practical man. A boy
could scarcely grow up on the Illinois frontier and
not be practical—otherwise he would not grow up
very far! Slavery was wrong, and the sight of slaves
made him miserable. But what was Lincoln to do
about it?

It would not help very much to call Southerners
hard names. No one mends his ways because he is

called names. It certainly would not help to try to steal their slaves away from them. Some Northerners did, and set them free, one by one. That only made the masters more determined than ever to keep slavery as it was. And it made no dent on slavery at all.

But Lincoln did what he could—at least, so he thought. In 1846, his friends in Illinois sent him to the Congress in Washington. He hated to see the slave markets there, the buying and selling of black men and women and children in the very shadow of the Capitol. Besides, what would foreign diplomats and visitors think of that spectacle in this "land of the free"?

Lincoln worked out a scheme to end slavery in the District of Columbia. He thought the government could buy up all the slaves and then set them free. Nothing came of this scheme at the time, but Lincoln did not forget it. Later he went back to it.

He was one of those, too, who tried to prevent slavery from flooding over its existing limits into the new territory in the West—territory just being opened for settlement. For, as he said a little later:

The whole nation is interested that the best use shall be made of these territories. We want them for homes of free white people. Slave states are places for poor white people to remove from, not to remove to. New free states are the places for poor people to go to, and better their

20

condition. For this use the nation needs these territories.

This, as Lincoln saw it, was the practical issue: to keep slavery from spreading, to keep the West as a home for "free men." All through the 1850's, as Lincoln took a more and more prominent place on the national stage, he discussed and debated this issue. These were the years when the railroads at last reached the Mississippi. These were the years when thousands and thousands of eager settlers were moving out over the rich prairie soil of Iowa and Kansas and Nebraska. Should this vast new West be slave or free?

It was the great question of the 'fifties. Southerners, naturally enough, said that the West should be slave. Hundreds of them set out to make it slave—by

Lincoln addressing the court in Shelbyville, Illinois, June 15, 1856.

force if necessary. Northerners said it should be free. From all over the Middle West, and from far-distant New England, settlers went off to Kansas to take up land and to fight for freedom. Some of them sang that new song by John Greenleaf Whittier:

> We cross the prairies as of old
> The pilgrims crossed the sea,
> To make the West as they the east
> The homestead of the free.

Soon there was a small-scale war going on—a war that threatened to grow into a big war, unless something was done about it.

It all came to a head in 1858, in a famous series of debates between Lincoln and Stephen A. Douglas, the Senator from Illinois. There was no one quite like Douglas, no one so smart, or so famous, or so sure of himself. He was known as the "Little Giant," and he could take on all comers.

Lincoln debating with Stephen A. Douglas.

In 1858, Douglas took on Abraham Lincoln, who wanted his place in the United States Senate. All that summer and fall, the two of them were at it hammer and tongs. They spoke in one little hot, straggling Illinois town after another. The dust of hundreds of wagons was in the air; and the sun broiled down on thousands of tough, gnarled, hard-working farmers, and their wives and children, too, who came to hear them.

It was slavery the two men argued about, slavery in the territories now open to settlement. But, as often happens when we talk about anything long enough and hard enough, the argument changed and took on a new character.

The campaign itself changed. Lincoln and Douglas had started campaigning for a seat in the Senate. Before they were through, both of them were thinking about the Presidency, and campaigning for a nomination that was two years off.

The subject of the debates changed. The tall, leathery Lincoln and the short, polished Douglas had begun talking about slavery in the territories. Before long, they were down to bedrock, talking about the rights and wrongs of slavery itself.

It was natural enough. If a person feels that slavery is a good thing, or if he doesn't really care one way or another, then he doesn't mind if it spreads into new territory. That was pretty much what Senator Douglas felt. But if—like Lincoln—a man

23

thinks slavery is an evil and a curse, then he minds very much if it spreads.

Here is the way Lincoln put the matter in his speech at Galesburg, Illinois:

I suppose that the real difference between Judge Douglas and his friends and the Republicans . . . is that the judge is not in favor of making any difference between slavery and liberty . . . and consequently every sentiment he utters discards the idea that there is any wrong in slavery. . . .

If you will take the judge's speeches, and select the short and pointed sentences expressed by him—as his declaration that he "don't care whether slavery is voted up or down"—you will see that this is perfectly logical, if you do not admit that slavery is wrong. If you do admit that it is wrong, Judge Douglas cannot logically say that he don't care whether a wrong is voted up or voted down.

Judge Douglas declares that if any community wants slavery, they have a right to have it. He can say that logically, if he says there is no wrong in slavery. But if you admit that there is a wrong in it, he cannot logically say that anybody has a right to do wrong. . . .

Now, I confess myself to belong to that class

Lincoln and Douglas at Galesburg, Illinois.

in the country who contemplate slavery as a moral, social, and political evil, and who desire a policy that looks to the prevention of it as a wrong, and looks hopefully to the time when as a wrong it may come to an end.

Just a week later, Lincoln and Douglas went over to the little town of Alton, on the Mississippi River, and took up the same subject. This time, Lincoln talked about what he called "the real issue":

> Judge Douglas says that, upon the score of equality, slaves should be allowed to go into a new territory like any other property. This is strictly logical if there is no difference between it and other property. If it and other property are equal, his argument is entirely logical. But if you insist that one is wrong and the other right, there is no use to institute a comparison between right and wrong. . . .
>
> That is the real issue. That is the issue that will continue in this country when these poor tongues of Judge Douglas and myself shall be silent. It is the eternal struggle between these two principles—right and wrong—throughout the world. They are the two principles that have stood face to face from the beginning of time; and will ever continue to struggle.
>
> The one is the common right of humanity, and the other the divine right of kings. It is the same principle in whatever shape it develops itself. It is the same spirit that says, "You toil and work and earn bread, and I'll eat it." No matter in what shape it comes, whether from the mouth of a king who seeks to bestride the people of his own nation and live by the fruit of their labor, or from one race of men as an apol-

FREE SPEECH.
FREE HOMES.
FREE TERRITORY.

PROTECTION
TO
AMERICAN
INDUSTRY

FOR PRESIDENT
ℝAHAM LINCOLN
OF ILLINOIS

FOR VICE PRESIDENT
HANNIBAL HAMLIN
OF MAINE

Election poster for Lincoln and Hannibal Hamlin.

ogy for enslaving another race, it is the same tyrannical principle. . . .

And whenever we can get rid of the fog which obscures the real question—when we can get Judge Douglas and his friends to avow a policy looking to its perpetuation—we can get out from among them that class of men and bring them to the side of those who treat it as a wrong. Then there will soon be an end of it, and that end will be its "ultimate extinction."

27

Senator Douglas won that election to the Senate —by the narrowest possible margin. But both Douglas and Lincoln were looking forward to a much more important election: the Presidential election of 1860. Sure enough, in 1860, the Democrats named Douglas their candidate, and the Republicans named Lincoln.

When all the votes were counted, it was found that this time Lincoln had come in well ahead of Douglas. He had won the biggest of all elections—election to the Presidency of the whole United States.

The Inauguration of

But, alas, when Lincoln went from his home in Springfield to Washington, to take the oath of office, the United States was not whole any more. The question of slavery had split the nation in two. Now it was North and South, the Union and the Confederacy, the Blue and the Gray.

Southerners wanted to keep slavery. Their way of

28

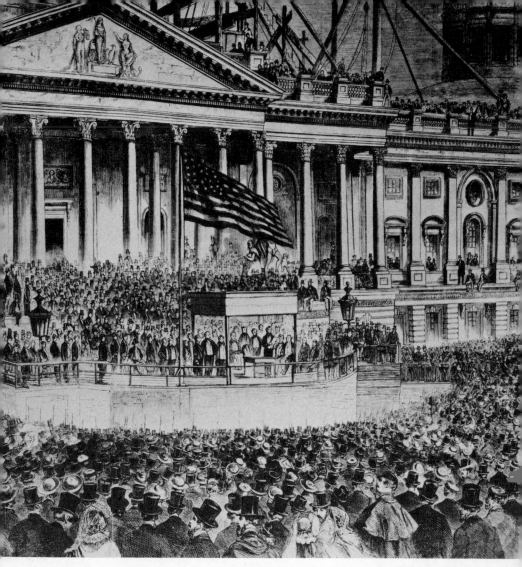

the Sixteenth President, March 4, 1861.

life was woven into slavery, and, indeed, based upon it. They feared that Lincoln and the North would not let them live their own way. Were they right or wrong in this? Who knows? Anyway, that was the way they felt. As soon as Lincoln had been elected President, they hurried out of the Union, and set up

29

housekeeping—or "statekeeping"—on their own. Soon they were all singing a new song:

> First, gallant South Carolina
> Nobly made the stand;
> Then came Alabama,
> Who took her by the hand.
> All raised the flag, the bonnie blue flag
> That bears a single star.

Carolina, and Alabama, and Mississippi, and Georgia, and Louisiana, and Florida, and Arkansas, and after them four other Southern states—eleven in all! Poor Abraham Lincoln! He went to Washington and found that half of the country would not recognize him as President at all. Worse still, he soon had a war on his hands.

The war started with a polite little argument in the harbor of Charleston, South Carolina. It grew and grew until it became the biggest and most terrible war in the whole of American history!

What was it all about? Why did Americans, who had got along well together for a hundred years and more, suddenly start to fight each other and to kill each other?

This Civil War, or War Between the States, was about two things. It was about the Union, and about Slavery—and the two were joined together as closely

as the two sides of one's hand. Because the Southerners wanted to keep slavery, they left the Union.
Because Lincoln was determined to save the Union,
he found, in the end, that he had to get rid of slavery.

II

WHAT DID slavery have to do with saving the Union?
Everything. At least, so Lincoln came to believe.

Though the slaves did not fight in the Confederate
ranks, they did the work behind the lines that made it
possible for their masters to go off and fight. They
did the work: they raised the food, they tended the
horses and the cattle, they took care of the homes and
kept things going.

Even this was not the most important reason for
freeing the slaves. Most important was the effect it
would have everywhere in the world. It would make
this war a war for freedom. That was something
even the simplest folks could understand—freedom.

Army of the Potomac—Negro baggage drivers watering their mules.

Men and women throughout the North who had worked and prayed so long for the end of slavery could understand it. Even those who had not bothered much, one way or another, about the poor Negro could understand it. The boys in blue were tramping off to camp with a new marching song:

> Yes, we'll rally round the flag, boys,
> We'll rally once again,
> Shouting the battle cry of Freedom!

It was a good battle cry, none better. But even that was not enough. Soon people in the North were given a new song of freedom. Julia Ward Howe, the wife of a famous Abolitionist, wrote "The Battle Hymn of the Republic." Mrs. Howe tells us how she came to write it:

We were invited one day to attend a review of troops at some distance from the town [of Washington]. . . . We returned to the city very slowly, for the troops nearly filled the road. My dear minister was in the carriage with me, as were several other friends. To beguile the rather tedious drive, we sang from time to time snatches of the army songs so popular at that time, concluding with:

"John Brown's body lies a-mouldering in
        the ground;
    His soul is marching on."

The soldiers seemed to like this and answered back, "Good for you."

Mr. Clark said, "Mrs. Howe, why do you not write some good words for that stirring tune?"

I replied that I had often wished to do this, but had not as yet found in my mind any leading to it.

I went to bed that night as usual and slept, according to my wont, quite soundly. I awoke in the gray of the morning twilight, and as I lay

35

waiting for the dawn, the long lines of the desired poem began to twine themselves in my mind. Having thought out all the stanzas, I said to myself, "I must get up and write these verses down, lest I fall asleep again and forget them."

So with a sudden effort I sprang out of bed and found in the dimness an old stump of a pen which I remembered to have used the day before. I scrawled the verses almost without looking at the paper. I had learned to do this when on previous occasions, attacks of versification had visited me in the night. . . . Having completed my writing, I returned to bed and fell asleep, saying to myself, "I like this better than most things that I have written."

The poem . . . soon found its way to the camps, as I heard from time to time of its being sung in chorus by the soldiers.

Here is what Mrs. Howe wrote in the dim shadows of that morning:

Mine eyes have seen the glory of the coming of
    the Lord;
He is trampling out the vintage where the grapes
    of wrath are stored;
He hath loosed the fateful lightning of His terrible, swift sword;
        His truth is marching on.

Julia Ward Howe

I have seen Him in the watch fires of a hundred
    circling camps;
They have builded Him an altar in the evening
    dews and damps;
I can read His righteous sentence by the dim and
    flaring lamps.
        His day is marching on.

37

The Army of the Cumberland—Missionary Ridge.

I have read a fiery gospel writ in burnished rows
    of steel;
"As ye deal with My contemners, so with you
    My grace shall deal;
Let the Hero, born of woman, crush the serpent
    with His heel,
        Since God is marching on."

He has sounded forth the trumpet that shall
    never call retreat;
He is sifting out the hearts of men before His
    judgment seat;
Oh, be swift, my soul, to answer Him! be jubi-
    lant, my feet!
        Our God is marching on.

In the beauty of the lilies Christ was born across
    the sea,
With a glory in His bosom that transfigures you
    and me;
As He died to make men holy, let us die to make
    men free,
        While God is marching on.

"As He died to make men holy, let us die to make men free." That was a message the soldiers could understand—and the folks back home, as well.

The English, too, could understand it. That was important; because if England should come in on the side of the South, the war might go on forever. Many of the English were not quite sure what the American war was all about—it is always hard to understand other people's wars!

Besides, some of the people in England, especially the rich and the powerful, favored the South. It was not that they approved of slavery. It was, rather, that they did not like democracy very much—not Lincoln's brand of democracy, anyway. Lincoln thought that everybody was as good as anybody, and anybody as good as everybody. The aristocratic English were afraid of this idea. They knew that if it won out in America, it might spread to the Old World, and that would be the end of them.

On the other hand, the workingmen and women of England did believe in democracy, and in equality.

They knew a real democrat when they saw one—and when they looked across the Atlantic at Abraham Lincoln, they saw one. They had no use for the South, or for slavery. And it was important to make it clear to them that they had a stake in the American war, a stake in Union victory. It was important to show them that both democracy and freedom were all tied up in Union victory.

Lincoln tried to make this clear in his very first message to Congress—a message really directed to all the world:

> This is essentially a people's contest. On the side of the Union, it is a struggle for maintaining in the world that form and substance of government whose leading object is to elevate the condition of men—to lift artificial weights from all shoulders, to clear the paths of laudable pursuit for all, to afford all an unfettered start, and a fair chance in the race of life.

The English workingmen could understand this language. They understood, too, the language of freedom.

But, of course, the Negroes themselves could understand freedom best of all.

Southerners would not—or could not—use their slaves to fight in their armies. It would be quite foolish to expect anyone to fight for the right to be a slave! Lincoln had no such troubles, though. If the Negro would not fight to be a slave, he *would* fight in order to be free. If Lincoln once made it clear that the war was for *freedom*, he could count on the Negro to help.

And help he did. Before the war was over, almost 200,000 Negroes wore the Union blue. They stormed the batteries in Charleston Harbor. They fought on gunboats nosing their way up the winding streams of Florida. They fought in distant Missouri and all along the Mississippi River, and in the bayous of Louisiana. They served behind the lines in Virginia and Tennessee. Wherever there was work to do, or fighting to do, there they were.

"If all earthly power were given me," Lincoln had

Negro recruits at Charleston, South Carolina.

Culver Service

said, "I should not know what to do" about slavery. Now power was given him—not all earthly power, perhaps, but such power as no other American President ever had before. Better yet, wisdom was given him, for who was wiser or more just than Lincoln? Gradually, he came to see what he had to do to save the Union. He had to free the slaves!

Lincoln's first idea was the same one he had had as a Congressman, almost twenty years earlier. He would buy the freedom of the slaves. To be sure, it was very unlikely that the slave-holders of the Confederacy would listen for a moment to such an idea. They intended to win the war—and to keep their slaves, thank you!

However, in the states along the border between the North and the South, that were still in the Union, there were half a million slaves. Why not *pay* the slave-owners in these states to free their slaves? What a wonderful idea!

The plan would be fair to the slave-holders who were loyal to the Union. It would show that slavery *could* be ended peacefully, if only people would listen to reason and common sense. It would show that all this bloodshed and killing was not necessary. The end of the war would soon come. And hundreds of thousands of Negro slaves would be free.

First, Lincoln turned to the Border States themselves. "Oh, how I wish they would accept my proposition," he said to his old friend, Owen Love-

42

joy. "Then you and all of us would not have lived in vain."

He invited the leaders of the three great Border States—Maryland, Kentucky and Missouri—to the White House, and laid his plan before them. "I beseech you," he said, "to make the arguments for yourselves; you cannot, if you would, be blind to the signs of the times." If freedom came in this way, "it would come gently, as the dews from heaven, not rending or wrecking anything. Will you not embrace it?"

No, they would not! For whatever reason, out of whatever folly, they would not!

Then, Lincoln turned to Congress, and asked them to take the lead in this scheme of buying freedom for the slaves. He argued, he reasoned, he begged; and he closed with a moving appeal:

Fellow citizens, *we* cannot escape history. We of this Congress and this Administration will be remembered in spite of ourselves. No personal significance or insignificance can spare one or another of us. The fiery trial through which we pass will light us down, in honor or dishonor, to the latest generation.

We *say* we are for the Union. The world will not forget that we say this. We know how to save the Union. The world knows we do know how to save it.

We, even *we here*, hold the power and bear the responsibility. In giving freedom to the slave, we assure freedom to the free—honorable alike in what we give and what we preserve. We shall nobly save or meanly lose the last, best hope of earth. Others may succeed; this could not fail. The way is plain, peaceful, generous, just—

Lincoln frees the slaves in Washington.

a way which, if followed, the world will forever applaud, and God must forever bless.

"Other means may succeed; this could not fail!" Perhaps not, but it was not to be tried. Congress did not co-operate; the Border States did not co-operate. A small dent was made in slavery, to be sure: Congress bought and freed the slaves in Washington, itself. That scandal, at least, was ended—the scandal Lincoln had wanted to end long ago, when he was an unknown Congressman.

But, as for slavery itself, it was now up to Lincoln to try "other means."

III

EARLY in the year 1862, the Union Navy steamed up the mouth of the Mississippi River. They bombarded a few Confederate forts that tried to stop them, and sailed on to take the great city of New Orleans. Soon the Stars and Stripes waved over most of Louisiana.

That July, a Louisiana slave-holder sat down and wrote a letter to President Lincoln. Did the President know how harsh the war was? he asked. Did Lincoln know how much suffering it cost the poor Southerners? Did he know that the Union Army was taking slaves away from their rightful owners? Couldn't he do something to stop this outrage?

Busy as he was, Lincoln took time to answer this

curious letter. War is war, he said. And, after all, who started it, anyway? If the people of Louisiana rise up against the Union, they must take the consequences. One of the consequences was that when the Union Army arrived, slaves would run away. Did Southerners suppose the Army had fought its way there just to *strengthen* slavery? Lincoln went on to ask:

What would you do in my position? Would you drop the war where it is? Or would you prosecute it in the future with elder-stalk squirts charged with rose water?

That same month, Lincoln was getting ready to take the whole question of slavery into his own hands—and settle it. Things were going badly on the battlefield. The Confederate General Robert E. Lee had just whipped the Union Army near Richmond and sent it scurrying back to Washington. Now Lee was on the offensive, the mighty Lee who dealt such hammer blows. No wonder Lincoln felt that the time had come for drastic action.

One torrid day in mid-July (and Washington in July can be hotter than the Sahara Desert), Lincoln called for his carriage in order to attend a funeral. He invited two of his old friends to go with him: William E. Seward, the shrewd little wizard who ran

General Robert Edward Lee

the State Department; and big, lumbering Gideon
Welles, the Secretary of the Navy, who hid himself
behind an immense bouquet of whiskers.

Welles—bless him—kept a diary, and in it he wrote
down what the President had said during that buggy
ride:

It was on this ride that [President Lincoln] first

49

mentioned to Mr. Seward and myself the subject of emancipating the slaves by proclamation in case the Rebels did not cease . . . in their war on the Government and the Union. . . . He dwelt earnestly on the gravity, importance, and delicacy of the movement, said he had given it much thought and had about come to the conclusion that it was a military necessity . . . that we must free the slaves or be ourselves subdued, etc., etc.

This was, he said, the first occasion upon which he had mentioned the subject to anyone, and wished us to frankly state how the proposition struck us. . . .

Two or three times on that ride the subject, which was of course an absorbing one for each and all, was adverted to, and, before separating, the President desired us to give the question special and deliberate attention, for he was earnest in the conviction that something must be done. . . .

The slaves, if not armed and disciplined, were in the service of those who were, not only as field laborers and producers, but thousands of them were in attendance upon the armies in the field, employed as waiters and teamsters; and the fortifications and intrenchments were constructed by them.

This was the first hint President Lincoln had given

of what he planned to do. Lincoln had already made up his mind what to do, but he was not yet quite sure how to do it, or when. He thought about it, whenever he could; he worked at it, whenever he had time.

The White House was not a very good place for thinking or working. People swarmed into it all day long. Everyone wanted to see the President: a general to talk over the war, an office-seeker to get a job, a delegation to complain about some policy or other, a foreign visitor who wanted only to see what Lincoln looked like, a mother to ask a pardon for her soldier son who had slept on sentry duty.

When he wanted quiet, Lincoln used to escape to the Telegraph Office in the War Department, just across the street. Major Eckert, the Superintendent of Military Telegraph, remembered how the President had come, day after day, to work on a secret paper:

The President came to the office every day, and invariably sat at my desk while there. Upon his arrival early one morning in June, 1862, shortly after McClellan's Seven Days' Battles, he asked me for some paper, as he wanted to write something special. I procured some foolscap and handed it to him. He then sat down and began to write. I do not recall whether the sheets were loose or had been made into a pad. There must have been at least a quire.

51

He would look out of the window a while and then put his pen to paper, but he did not write much at once. He would study between times, and when he had made up his mind he would put down a line or two, and then sit quiet for a few minutes. After a time, he would resume his writing, only to stop again at intervals to make some remark to me or to one of the cipher operators as a fresh dispatch from the front was handed to him.

Once his eyes were arrested by the sight of a

President Lincoln writes the first draft of the Emancipation Proclamation.

large spiderweb stretched from the lintel of the portico to the side of the outer window sill.

This spider web was an institution of the cipher room and harbored a large colony of exceptionally big ones. We frequently watched their antics, and Assistant Secretary Watson dubbed them "Major Eckert's lieutenants." Lincoln commented on the web, and I told him my lieutenants would soon report and pay their respects to the President.

Not long after, a big spider appeared at the crossroads and tapped several times on the strands, whereupon five or six others came out from different directions. Then what seemed to be a great confab took place, after which they separated, each on a different strand of the web. Lincoln was much interested in the performance, and thereafter, while working at the desk, would often watch for the appearance of his visitors.

On the first day, Lincoln did not cover one sheet of his special writing paper (nor indeed on any subsequent day). When ready to leave, he asked me to take charge of what he had written and not allow anyone to see it. I told him I would do this with pleasure, and would not read it myself.

"Well," he said, "I should be glad to know that no one will see it, although there is no objection to your looking at it. But please keep it locked up until I call for it tomorrow."

I said his wishes would be strictly complied with.

When he came to the office on the following day he asked for the papers, and I unlocked my desk and handed them to him, and he again sat down to write. This he did nearly every day for several weeks, always handing me what he had written when ready to leave the office each day.

Sometimes he could not write more than a line or two, and once I observed that he had put question marks on the margin of what he had written. He would read over each day all the matter he had previously written, and revise it, studying carefully each sentence.

On one occasion, he took the papers with him, but he brought them back a day or two later. I became much interested in the matter, and was impressed with the idea that he was engaged upon something of great importance, but I did not know what it was until he had finished the document. . . . Then for the first time he told me that he had been writing an order giving freedom to the slaves in the South, for the purpose of ending the war.

By July 22, Lincoln had finished his paper. He called a meeting of his Cabinet, to read them what he had written, and to hear what they had to say about it. Lincoln himself told the story to Frank Carpenter, an artist who had come to paint his picture:

It had got to be midsummer, 1862. Things had gone on from bad to worse, until I felt that we had reached the end of our rope on the plan of operations we had been pursuing; that we had about played our last card, and must change our tactics or lose the game!

I now determined upon the adoption of the emancipation policy; and, without consultation with, or knowledge of the Cabinet, I prepared the original draft of the proclamation and, after much anxious thought, called a Cabinet meeting upon the subject. This was the last of July or the first part of August, 1862 (the exact date, he did not remember).

This Cabinet meeting took place, I think, upon a Saturday. All were present, excepting Mr. Blair, the Postmaster-General, who was absent at the opening of the discussion, but came in subsequently. I said to the Cabinet that I had resolved upon this step, and had not called them together to ask their advice but to lay the subject matter of the proclamation before them, suggestions as to which would be in order after they had heard it read. . . .

Reading the first draft, July 22, 1862.

Then the President read them his draft of the Proclamation. When he had finished—

Various suggestions were offered. Secretary Chase wished the language stronger in reference to the arming of the blacks. Mr. Blair, after he came in, deprecated the policy on the ground that it would cost the Administration the fall elections. Nothing, however, was offered that I had not already fully anticipated and settled in my own mind, until Secretary Seward spoke.

He said in substance: "Mr. President, I approve of the proclamation but I question the expediency of its issue at this juncture. The depression of the public mind, consequent upon our repeated reverses, is so great that I fear the effect of so important a step. It may be viewed as the last measure of an exhausted government, a cry for help; the government stretching forth its hand to Ethiopia instead of Ethiopia stretching forth her hands to the government."

His idea was that it would be considered our last *shriek* on the retreat. (This was his precise expression.)

"Now," continued Mr. Seward, "while I approve the measure, I suggest, sir, that you postpone its issue until you can give it to the country supported by military success, instead of issuing it, as would be the case now, upon the greatest disasters of the war!"

The wisdom of the view of the Secretary of State struck me with very great force. It was an aspect of the case that, in all my thought upon the subject, I had entirely overlooked. The result was that I put the draft of the proclamation aside, as you do your sketch for a picture, waiting for victory.

From time to time I added or changed a line, touching it up here and there, anxiously watching the progress of events. Well, the next news we had was of Pope's disaster at Bull Run. Things looked darker than ever. Finally came the week of the battle of Antietam. I determined to wait no longer.

"The week of Antietam . . ." Lee had whipped McClellan in front of Richmond. Then he had turned North, beaten another Union general—the unlucky John Pope—and sent his army reeling back to Washington. Now, flushed with victory, the great Lee was determined to bring the war home to the people of the North, as they had brought it home to the people of the South.

Tramp, tramp, tramp along the dusty roads of Virginia went the Confederate Army. Splashing across the shallow waters of the Potomac, and scrabbling up the Maryland shore and into Maryland, they sang:

> Thou wilt not cower in the dust,
> Maryland!
> Thy gleaming sword shall never rust,
> Maryland!
> Remember Carroll's sacred trust,
> Remember Howard's warlike thrust,
> And all thy slumberers with the just,
> Maryland! My Maryland!

At the little village of Sharpsburg, on Antietam Creek, the Union Army caught up with Lee. All day long, in that golden mid-September, the two great

58

By the President of the
United States of America
A Proclamation

I Abraham Lincoln, President of the United States of America, and Commander-in Chief of the Army and Navy thereof, do hereby proclaim and declare that hereafter, as heretofore, the war will be prosecuted for the object of practically restoring the constitutional relation between the United States, and each of the states, and the people thereof, in which states that relation is, or may be suspended, or disturbed.

That it is my purpose, upon the next meeting of Congress to again recommend the adoption of a practical measure tendering pecuniary aid to the free acceptance or rejection of all slave-states, so called, the people whereof may not then be in rebellion against the United States, and which states, may then have voluntarily adopted, or thereafter may voluntarily adopt, immediate, or gradual abolishment of slavery within their respective limits; and that the effort to colonize persons of African descent upon this continent, or elsewhere, will be continued.

Preliminary Proclamation of September 22, 1862.

armies fought back and forth through the wheat fields and the orchards of that lovely countryside. The waters of the little creek ran red with blood.

When it was over, both armies still stood their ground. But the next day, Lee pulled out and headed back to Virginia. The invasion was over, and Lincoln could claim a victory.

That was what he had been waiting for, and a long wait it had been. By now, he had finished and polished the great state paper he had been working on for so long. He was prepared to read it to his Cabinet again—and to issue it to the public. On September 22, just a few days after the news of Antietam had reached him, he called a meeting of the Cabinet.

Two of the Cabinet members kept diaries, so we have a record of everything that happened at that famous meeting. One of them was the Secretary of the Treasury, Salmon Chase. He was a big, self-important man, who wanted very much to be President himself. But he was loyal to Lincoln. The other man was Gideon Welles, whom we have already met on a buggy ride with the President. Here is how Secretary Chase remembered the Cabinet meeting:

September 22, 1862. To department about nine. State Department messenger came with notices to heads of departments to meet at twelve. Received sundry callers. Went to the White House.

First reading of the Emancipation Proclamation.

All the members of the Cabinet were in attendance. There was some general talk, and the President mentioned that Artemus Ward had sent him his book. Proposed to read a chapter which he thought very funny. Read it, and seemed to enjoy it very much; the heads also (except Stanton). The chapter was "High-handed Outrage at Utica."

The President then took a graver tone and said: "Gentlemen, I have, as you are aware, thought a great deal about the relation of this war to slavery, and you all remember that, several weeks ago, I read to you an order I had pre-

Salmon P. Chase,
Secretary of the Treasury

Gideon Welles,
Secretary of the Navy

pared upon the subject, which, on account of objections made by some of you, was not issued. Ever since then my mind has been much occupied with this subject, and I have thought all along that the time for acting on it might probably come.

"I think the time has come now. I wish it was a better time. I wish that we were in a better condition. The action of the army against the rebels has not been quite what I should have liked best. But they have been driven out of Maryland, and Pennsylvania is no longer in danger of invasion.

"When the rebel army was at Frederick, I

determined, as soon as it should be driven out of Maryland, to issue a proclamation of emancipation such as I thought most likely to be useful. I said nothing to anyone, but I made a promise to myself and (hesitating a little) to my Maker.

"The rebel army is now driven out, and I am going to fulfill that promise. I have got you together to hear what I have written down. I do not wish your advice about the main matter, for that I have determined for myself. This I say without intending anything but respect for any one of you. But I already know the views of each on this question. They have been heretofore expressed, and I have considered them as thoroughly and carefully as I can.

"What I have written is that which my reflections have determined me to say. If there is anything in the expressions I use, or in any minor matter, which any one of you thinks had best be changed, I shall be glad to receive your suggestions.

"One other observation I will make. I know very well that many others might, in this matter as in others, do better than I can. And if I was satisfied that the public confidence was more fully possessed by any one of them than by me, and knew of any constitutional way in which he could be put in my place, he should have it. I would gladly yield it to him.

"But, though I believe that I have not so much of the confidence of the people as I had some time since, I do not know that, all things considered, any other person has more. And however this may be, there is no way in which I can have any other man put where I am. I am here. I must do the best I can and bear the responsibility of taking the course which I feel I ought to take."

The President then proceeded to read his Emancipation Proclamation, making remarks on the several parts as he went on, and showing that he had fully considered the subject in all the lights under which it had been presented to him.

After he had closed, Governor Seward said: "The general question having been decided, nothing can be said further about that. Would it not, however, make the proclamation more clear and decided to leave out all reference to the act being sustained during the incumbency of the present President; and not merely say that the Government 'recognizes' but that it will maintain the freedom it proclaims?"

I followed, saying: "What you have said, Mr. President, fully satisfies me that you have given to every proposition, which has been made, a kind and candid consideration. And you have now expressed the conclusion to which you have arrived clearly and distinctly. This it was your

William H. Seward,
Secretary of State

right and, under your oath of office, your duty to do.

"The proclamation does not, indeed, mark out the course I would myself prefer; but I am ready to take it just as it is written and to stand by it with all my heart. I think, however, the suggestions of Governor Seward very judicious, and shall be glad to have them adopted."

The President then asked us severally our opinions as to the modifications proposed, saying that he did not care much about the phrases he had used. Every one favored the modification, and it was adopted.

Governor Seward then proposed that in the passage relating to colonization, some language should be introduced to show that the colonization proposed was to be only with the consent of the colonists, and the consent of the states in which the colonies might be attempted. This, too, was agreed to.

Seward's two suggestions did not amount to much. After he had accepted them, Lincoln looked at Seward with a lift of his eyebrows, and said, "Why didn't you make both those suggestions at once?"

It reminded him, he added, of the hired man out in Illinois who came to the farmer one day and told him that one of a yoke of oxen had dropped dead. Then, after a long wait, the hired man told him that the other ox had dropped dead, too.

"Why didn't you tell me at once that both oxen were dead?" the farmer asked.

"Because," said the hired man, "I didn't want to hurt your feelings by telling you too much at one time."

Gideon Welles did not seem to remember about Lincoln's reading the "High-handed Outrage at Utica," or the story of the Illinois farmer. Perhaps he thought these things were not dignified enough to put down in his diary.

However, he did remember a few other things that Chase did not mention. Most interesting is Lincoln's confession that he had made a vow to God to free the slaves, if God gave the Union victory. Lincoln regarded what he was now doing as an expression of the Divine will. But, let Welles tell his own story:

September 22. A special Cabinet meeting. The subject was the Proclamation for emancipating the slaves after a certain date, in states that shall then be in rebellion. For several weeks, the subject has been suspended, but, the President says, never lost sight of. . . .

Now, taking up the Proclamation, the President stated that the question was finally decided, the act and the consequences were his, but that he felt it due to us to make us acquainted with the fact and to invite criticism on the paper which he had prepared.

There were, he had found . . . some differences in the Cabinet, but he had, after ascertaining in his own way the views of each and all . . . formed his own conclusions and made his own decisions.

In the course of the discussion on this paper, which was long, earnest, and . . . harmonious, he remarked that he had made a vow, a covenant, that if God gave us the victory in the approaching battle, he would consider it an indication of Divine will, and that it was his duty to move forward in the cause of emancipation.

It might be thought strange, he said, that he had in this way submitted the disposal of mat-

ters, when the way was not clear to his mind what he should do. God had decided this question in favor of the slaves. He was satisfied it was right, was confirmed and strengthened in his action by the vow and the results.

His mind was fixed, his decision made, but he wished his paper announcing his course as correct in terms as it could be made, without any change in his determination. He read the document. One or two unimportant amendments suggested by Seward were approved. It was then handed to the Secretary of State to publish tomorrow . . . .

The question of power, authority, in the government to set free the slaves was not much discussed at this meeting, but had been canvassed by the President in private conversation with the members individually. Some thought legislation advisable before the step was taken, but Congress was clothed with no authority on this subject, nor is the Executive, except under the war power. . . .

It is momentous, both in its immediate and remote results, and an exercise of extraordinary power which cannot be justified on mere humanitarian principles, and would never have been attempted but to preserve the national existence.

The slaves must be with us or against us in

the war. Let us have them. These were my convictions, and this the drift of the discussion.

On the morning of the twenty-fourth, newspapers everywhere carried the glorious news that

> ... on the first day of January, A.D. 1863, all persons held as slaves within any state or designated part of a state, the people whereof shall then be in rebellion against the United States, shall be then, henceforward, and forever free.

There was excitement, there was rejoicing, there was hope. Little groups of Negroes and whites went around to serenade the President and members of the Cabinet.

Lincoln's private secretary, young John Hay, was at Secretary Chase's house. He reported that the serenaders came, and that Secretary Chase and Cassius Clay of Kentucky went out and made speeches to them. And "the crowd was in a glorious humor. ... They all seemed to feel a new and exhilarated life; they breathed freer. The President's proclamation had freed them, as well as the slaves."

That was one of the wonderful things about the Proclamation: it meant as much to the whites as to the Negroes. It lifted a burden from their hearts. It promised that they, too, would see a new dawn of freedom.

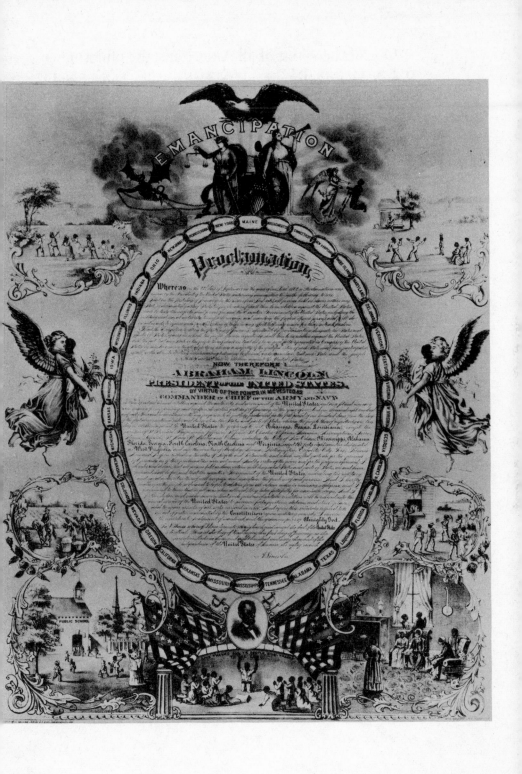

One of the wisest of all Americans, the philosopher Ralph Waldo Emerson, said this. He had already come to think of Lincoln as one of the great men of history. He saw that the war had to be a war for freedom, as well as a war for Union—a war for the freedom of all people, white as well as black.

Now, sitting up in his cold little study, in his house in Concord, Massachusetts, Emerson pondered the deeper meaning of Lincoln's promise to make the slaves "forever free."

A day which most of us dared not hope to see, an event worth the dreadful war . . . seems now to be close before us. October, November, December will have passed over beating hearts and plotting brains. Then the hour will strike, and all men of African descent who find their way to our lines are assured of the protection of American law.

It is by no means necessary that this measure should be suddenly marked by any signal results on the Negroes or on the Rebel masters. The force of the act is that it commits the country to this justice. . . . It is not a measure that admits of being taken back. Done, it cannot be undone. . . .

The act makes clear that the lives of our heroes have not been sacrificed in vain. It makes

72

Ralph Waldo Emerson

a victory of our defeats. Our hurts are healed.
The health of the nation is repaired.

With a victory like this, we can stand many
disasters. We have recovered ourselves from
our false position, and planted ourselves on a

law of Nature. It is well to delay the steamers at the wharves, until this edict could be put on board.

Happy are the young who find the pestilence cleansed out of the earth, leaving open to them an honest career. Happy the old, who see Nature purified before they depart. Do not let the dying die; hold them back to this world until you have charged their ear with this message to other spiritual societies!

"October, November, December . . . then the hour will strike." On that great day, the day so long awaited, Lincoln would sign his promise into law.

Finally, it was the first of January, 1863. All that morning, and far into the afternoon, Lincoln received the hundreds of callers who crowded into the White House to wish him a Happy New Year. Late in the afternoon, when the crowds had thinned out a little, Secretary Seward came to Lincoln with a copy of the Proclamation in its final form.

Lincoln read it over carefully:

. . . I, Abraham Lincoln, President of the United States, by virtue of the power in me vested as Commander-in-Chief of the Army and Navy of the United States . . . and as a fit and necessary war measure, . . . do, on this first day of January, in the year of our Lord 1863, and

74

in accordance with my purpose to do so . . . order and declare that all persons held as slaves within [the] designated states and parts of states are, and henceforward shall be, free; and that the Executive Government of the United States, including the military and naval authorities thereof, will recognize and maintain the freedom of said persons. . . .

Then he took a gold pen that Senator Charles Sumner had given to him, dipped it into his ink-pot, and got ready to sign. Turning to Secretary Seward, he said,

I never, in my life, felt more certain that I was doing right, than I do in signing this paper. But I have been receiving calls and shaking hands since eleven o'clock this morning, until my arm is stiff and numb. Now this signature will be closely examined, and if they find my hand trembled they will say, "he had some compunctions." But anyway, it is going to be done.

And with that, he signed his name, *Abraham Lincoln*.

IV

EVERYWHERE Negroes were waiting for the word that would set them free—that would set their people free.

New York, Buffalo, Pittsburgh, Washington—all saluted the event with salvos from one hundred guns.

Up in Boston, the colored people gathered for a night of song and celebration, of prayer and thanksgiving. All day, they had waited for the news of the signing of the Proclamation to come over the new telegraph wires. At last it came.

Frederick Douglass, the great leader of the Negroes, was there. He had been a slave, and had es-

Frederick Douglass

caped into freedom. He remembered how the word
came from Washington:

The effect of the announcement was startling
beyond description, and the scene was wild and
grand. Joy and gladness exhausted all forms of
expression, from shouts of praise to sobs and
tears. My old friend, Rue, a Negro preacher,
expressed the heartfelt emotion of the hour
when he led all voices in the anthem
"Sound the loud timbrel o'er Egypt's dark
      sea,
    Jehovah hath triumphed, his people are
      free."

78

In near-by Cambridge, the beloved poet, Henry Wadsworth Longfellow, wrote that it was "a beautiful day, full of sunshine, ending in a tranquil moonlight night."

But of all the places, it was in South Carolina that the Negroes celebrated most joyfully the "Day of Jubilee." All winter long, Negroes had been streaming onto the islands along the coast. There, on the Sea Islands, they found freedom under the Stars and Stripes. They had already created a little civilization for themselves.

It was there, too, that Lincoln had sent the first all-Negro regiment to fight for freedom. It was the famous Fifty-fourth Massachusetts, now renamed the First South Carolina Regiment. The Reverend Thomas Wentworth Higginson, who had long been a crusader for freedom, left his church in Worcester, up in Massachusetts, to become colonel of this regiment.

Colonel Higginson tells us how the soldiers of his regiment, and the colored men and women and children of the region he commanded, celebrated their day of freedom:

January 1, 1863 (evening). A happy New Year to civilized people—mere white folks. Our festival has come and gone, with perfect success, and our good General has been altogether satisfied.

Last night the great fires were kept smouldering in the pit, and the beeves were cooked more or less—chiefly more—during which time they had to be carefully watched, and the great spits turned by main force. Happy were the merry fellows who were permitted to sit up all night, and watch the glimmering flames that threw a thousand fantastic shadows among the great gnarled oaks. And such a chattering as I was sure to hear whenever I awoke that night! . . .

About ten o'clock, the people began to collect by land, and also by water, in steamers sent by General Saxton for the purpose. And from that time, all avenues of approach were thronged.

The multitude were chiefly colored women,

Celebration of Emancipation Day

Thomas Wentworth Higginson

with gay handkerchiefs on their heads, and a sprinkling of men, with that peculiarly respectable look which these people always have on Sundays and holidays. There were many white visitors also—ladies on horseback, and in carriages, superintendents and teachers, officers and cavalrymen.

Our companies were marched to the neighborhood of the platform, and allowed to sit or stand, as at the Sunday services. The platform was occupied by ladies and dignitaries, and by the band of the Eighth Maine, which kindly volunteered for the occasion. The colored people filled up all the vacant openings in the beautiful grove around, and there was a cordon of mounted visitors beyond.

Above [were] the great live-oak branches and their trailing moss; beyond the people, a glimpse of the blue river.

The services began at half past eleven o'clock, with prayer by our chaplain, Mr. Fowler. . . . Then the President's Proclamation was read, . . . a thing infinitely appropriate. . . . Then the colors were presented to us by the Reverend Mr. French, a chaplain who brought them from the donors in New York. All this was according to the program.

Then followed an incident so simple, so touching, so utterly unexpected and startling, that I can scarcely believe it on recalling, though it gave the keynote to the whole day.

The very moment the speaker had ceased, and just as I took and waved the flag, which now for the first time meant anything to these poor people, there suddenly arose, close beside the platform, a strong male voice (but rather cracked

Giving thanks for freedom.

and elderly), into which two women's voices
instantly blended, singing, as if by an impulse
that could no more be repressed than the morning note of the song sparrow—

> "My Country, 'tis of thee,
> Sweet land of liberty,
> Of thee I sing!"

People looked at each other, and then at us
on the platform, to see whence came this inter-
ruption, not set down in the bills. Firmly and
irrepressibly the quavering voices sang on,
verse after verse; others of the colored people
joined in. Some whites on the platform began,
but I motioned them to silence.

83

I never saw anything so electric; it made all other words cheap; it seemed the choked voice of a race at last unloosed. Nothing could be more wonderfully unconscious. Art could not have dreamed of a tribute to the day of jubilee that should be so affecting; history will not believe it. And when I came to speak of it, after it was ended, tears were everywhere. . . .

Just think of it! The first day they ever had a country, the first flag they had ever seen which promised anything to their people, and here, while mere spectators stood in silence, waiting for my stupid words, these simple souls burst out in their lay, as if they were by their own hearths at home!

When they stopped, there was nothing to do for it but to speak, and I went on. But the life of the whole day was in those unknown people's song.

A Philadelphia girl was another Negro to leave her home for the Sea Islands. Charlotte Forten wanted to help with the work of making the Negroes ready for freedom. She, too, wrote about the great day:

What a grand, glorious day this has been! The dawn of freedom which it heralds may not break upon us at once, but it will surely come, and sooner, I believe, than we have ever dared hope before. My soul is glad with exceeding great gladness.

Not only in the northern cities, or on the Sea Islands of South Carolina, was there rejoicing. People were happy even across the Atlantic Ocean, in England and in France, and wherever men loved freedom.

From the workingmen of England came a steady stream of messages—from Manchester and Birmingham, from Halifax and York, from Glasgow and Carlisle. They all said much the same thing: We will stand with you in the cause of freedom, no matter what the cost. Lincoln wrote a reply that was meant for all of them:

To the Workingmen of Manchester: I have the honor to acknowledge the receipt of the address and resolutions which you sent me. . . .

When I came, on the 4th of March, 1861, through a free election, to preside in the Government of the United States, the country was found at the verge of civil war. Whatever might have been the cause, or whosesoever the fault, one duty, paramount to all others, was before me, namely, to maintain and preserve at once the Constitution and the integrity of the Federal Republic. . . .

I have understood well that the duty of self-preservation rests solely with the American people; but I have at the same time been aware that favor or disfavor of foreign nations might have a material influence in enlarging or prolonging the struggle with disloyal men in which the country is engaged.

A fair examination of history has served to authorize a belief that the past actions and influences of the United States were generally regarded as having been beneficial toward mankind. I have, therefore, reckoned upon the forbearance of nations. . . .

It is now a pleasant duty to acknowledge the demonstration you have given of your desire that a spirit of amity and peace toward this country may prevail in the councils of your Queen, who is respected and esteemed in your own country only more than she is by the kindred nation which has its home on this side of the Atlantic.

I know and deeply deplore the sufferings which the workingmen at Manchester, and in all Europe, are called to endure in this crisis. It has been often and studiously represented that the attempt to overthrow this government, which was built upon the foundation of human rights, and to substitute for it one which should rest exclusively on the basis of human slavery, was likely to obtain the favor of Europe. Through the action of our disloyal citizens, the workingmen of Europe have been subjected to severe trials, for the purpose of forcing their sanction to that attempt.

Under the circumstances, I cannot but regard your decisive utterances upon the question as an instance of sublime Christian heroism which has not been surpassed in any age or in any country. It is indeed an energetic and re-inspiring assurance of the inherent power of truth and of the ultimate and universal triumph of justice, humanity and freedom.

Lincoln's words were clear enough: So far, America has been on the side of freedom, and the influence of America has been all for the good. Now, if the men of England will support the Union, the cause of freedom will continue to flourish. All mankind will benefit together from victory!

During the year 1863, the area of freedom grew larger and larger. The armies in blue pushed their way deeper and deeper into the South, freeing hundreds of thousands of slaves. The Confederates fought back gallantly—and fiercely. The tide of battle surged back and forth—now a Confederate victory, now a Union—until the first week in July. Then came the turning point of the war. In that week the Confederates lost two great battles. They never recovered from the loss.

The siege of Vicksburg,

In the West, they lost the fight for the fortress city of Vicksburg, high above the Mississippi. Now the Confederacy was cut in two. It meant, in the words of Lincoln, that the Father of Waters went once again unvexed to the sea.

In the East, the Confederates lost the furious battle that took its name from the little Pennsylvania town

Culver Service

June 27, 1863.

of Gettysburg. That battle swept up and down the
hills and fields and orchards of Gettysburg for three
terrible days. When the ten thousand Confederate
soldiers who had made a last desperate charge, with
Pickett, were reduced to five, the battle was over.
Lee withdrew from the fight, and from the North.

The sun of the Confederacy had passed its mid-

89

mark, and was now a setting sun. But for the two or three million Negroes still held in slavery, it meant a rising sun—a sun bright with the promise of freedom.

Lincoln had this idea in mind when, one chilly November day, he went to Gettysburg. He was to give a short talk at the dedication of the cemetery there—a cemetery where the thousands of soldiers in blue and in gray who had fallen in that battle were buried.

Lincoln came from Washington on the train, and re-worked his speech as he came. He was trying to find the perfect words for the idea he wanted to make clear. His secretary, John Hay, tells us about the ceremonies on that morning of the nineteenth of November:

In the morning, I got a beast and rode out with the President's suite to the cemetery in the procession. The procession formed itself in an orphanly sort of way, and moved out with very little help from anybody.

And after a little delay, Mr. Everett took his place on the stand; and Mr. Stockton made a prayer, which thought it was a perfect oration; and Mr. Everett spoke as he always does, perfectly—and the President, in a fine, free way, with more grace than is his wont, said his half dozen words of consecration, and the music wailed and we went home through crowded and cheering streets.

Here is what Lincoln said. We have heard it before; listen to it now with the ear of a bondsman yearning to be free. Read it now as a message of hope:

Fourscore and seven years ago, our fathers brought forth upon this continent a new nation, conceived in liberty and dedicated to the proposition that all men are created equal.

Now we are engaged in a great civil war, testing whether that nation—or any nation, so conceived and so dedicated—can long endure.

We are met on a great battlefield of that war. We are met to dedicate a portion of it as the final resting place of those who have given their lives that that nation might live.

It is altogether fitting and proper that we should do this.

But, in a larger sense, we cannot dedicate, we cannot consecrate, we cannot hallow, this ground. The brave men, living and dead, who struggled here, have consecrated it far above our power to add or to detract.

The world will very little note nor long remember what we say here; but it can never forget what they did here.

It is for us, the living, rather, to be dedicated

Address delivered at the dedication of the cemetery at Gettysburg.

Four score and seven years ago our fathers brought forth on this continent, a new nation, conceived in Liberty, and dedicated to the proposition that all men are created equal.

Now we are engaged in a great civil war, testing whether that nation, or any nation so conceived and so dedicated, can long endure. We are met on a great battlefield of that war. We have come to dedicate a portion of that field, as a final resting place for those who here gave their lives that that nation might live. It is altogether fitting and proper that we should do this.

But, in a larger sense, we can not dedicate — we can not consecrate — we can not hallow this ground. The brave men, living and dead, who struggled here, have consecrated it, far above our poor power to add or detract. The world will little note, nor long remember what we say here, but it can never forget what they did here. It is for us the living, rather, to be dedicated here to

the unfinished work which they who fou:
ght here have thus far so nobly advanced.
It is rather for us to be here dedicated to
the great task remaining before us — that
from these honored dead we take increased
devotion to that cause for which they gave
the last full measure of devotion — that
we here highly resolve that these dead shall
not have died in vain — that this nation,
under God, shall have a new birth of free=
dom — and that government of the people,
by the people, for the people, shall not per=
ish from the earth.

Abraham Lincoln.

November 19. 1863.

here to the unfinished work that they have thus
far so nobly carried on. It is, rather, for us to be
here dedicated to the great task remaining before
us; that from these honored dead we take increased devotion to that cause for which they
here gave the last full measure of devotion; that
we here highly resolve that these dead shall not
have died in vain—that this nation, under God,
shall have a new birth of freedom—and that
government of the people, by the people, for
the people, shall not perish from the earth.

V

ONE MORNING in April 1864, President Lincoln opened a letter from his friend, Mary Mann. She was the widow of the great Horace Mann, who had breathed new life into the schools of the nation. The letter contained a petition from two hundred little children of Boston. They asked the President to free all slave children right away.

Lincoln wrote back to Mrs. Mann at once:

Please tell these little people I am very glad their young hearts are so full of just and generous sympathy, and that while I have not the power to grant all they ask, I trust they will remember that God has, and that, as it seems, He will do it.

Yours truly,
A. LINCOLN

Certainly that was the way things looked in 1864. Everywhere, slaves were winning their freedom.

Thousands of them, protected by Union armies, had taken the roads leading to the North. Others flocked to the army camps, the men bringing along their wives and children. Many of these men went to work for the Union. They built army camps, or took care of the horses, or improved the muddy roads of the South over which the soldiers would have to march and pull heavy guns. A good many Negroes enlisted in the Army and proudly wore the Union blue.

Every now and then, someone would come up with the same idea: If Lincoln would only give these

The Second Louisiana Colored Regiment

Negroes back to their former masters, he might win support in the South. Thus the war would end more quickly! It was, of course, a foolish idea, and that is the way Lincoln treated it. To one visitor who brought up the matter, Lincoln said, with unusual heat:

There have been men who have proposed to me to return to slavery the black warriors of Port Hudson and Olustee [two battles where the Negroes fought with unusual bravery]. . . . I should be damned in time and in eternity for so doing. The world shall know that I will keep my faith to friends and enemies, come what will.

at Fort Hudson, May 27, 1863.

Whatever some of the Southerners might think, the Negroes knew that Lincoln would keep his faith.

That summer of 1864, Lincoln went down to see General Grant at his headquarters in Virginia. Here Grant was locked in a last, furious struggle with Lee's forces. While Lincoln was there, Grant suggested that they visit the Negro soldiers who had fought so courageously in the Battle of the Crater. It had been a battle below ground where thousands had been killed or wounded or captured.

Lincoln agreed at once. "I want to take a look at those boys," he said, and

I read with the greatest delight the account, given in Mr. Dana's despatch to the Secretary of War, of how gallantly they behaved. He said they took six out of the sixteen guns captured that day.

I was opposed on nearly every side when I first favored the raising of colored regiments, but they have proved their efficiency, and I am glad they have kept pace with the white troops in the recent assaults.

When we wanted every able-bodied man who could be spared to go to the front, and my opposers kept objecting to the Negroes, I used to tell them that at such times it was just as well to be a little color-blind.

Bettman Archive

Lincoln and his generals.

Lincoln and Grant soon reached the camp of the colored soldiers. Then, as one of Grant's aides tells us, there occurred "a scene which defied description."

99

They beheld for the first time the liberator of their race—the man who, by a stroke of his pen, had struck the shackles from the limbs of their fellow bondsmen and proclaimed liberty to the enslaved.

Always impressionable, the enthusiasm of the blacks now knew no limits. They cheered, laughed, cried, sang hymns of praise, and shouted in their Negro dialect, "God bress Massa Linkum!" "De Lord save Fader Abraham!" They crowded about him and fondled his horse. Some of them kissed his hands, while others ran off crying in triumph to their comrades that they had touched his clothes.

The President rode with bared head. The tears had started to his eyes, and his voice was so broken by emotion, that he could scarcely articulate the words of thanks and congratulation which he tried to speak to the humble and devoted men through whose ranks he rode. . . .

And now the victorious Northern armies were aiming one giant blow after another against the stricken South. Sherman was smashing through Georgia and on to the sea. Thomas was clearing out the West. Grant was hammering away at Lee, south of Richmond. The North was winning, and surely that would be the end of slavery!

But would it? Was the end of slavery that certain?

100

Almost, but not quite. There were still two things that worried Lincoln when he thought about the fate of the Negroes. First, he had freed the slaves as a *war* measure, using his *war* powers. But when the war was over—what then? Would war measures still hold good in time of peace?

The second problem was even more troublesome. What about the slaves in the loyal states of Maryland, Delaware, Kentucky and Missouri? Lincoln had never freed them. He was not at war with these states. He could not use his war powers to punish loyal men just because they owned slaves! Once the war was over, would there still be islands of slavery all along the border between the North and the South?

It would be much better to settle the whole question completely and finally. The way to do this was plain: It should be put into the Constitution that there should be no more slavery in our country.

During 1864, there had been talk about a constitutional amendment to do away with slavery, once and for all. In March of that year, the Senate actually passed such an amendment. But when the bill reached the lower House, it ran into trouble. There were still too many Congressmen who did not think Congress had the power to abolish slavery everywhere.

By now, Lincoln was determined to push ahead with this measure. He told the Republicans that they had to come out against slavery.

The Republicans had already named Lincoln for

the Presidency again in 1864. Now they wrote into their platform a statement that, as slavery is always and everywhere hostile to the principles of republican government, justice and the national welfare required that it be ended.

On that platform—and with Lincoln—the Republicans again won the election. When Congress met, the following December, they listened to a message from the President. There was no excuse, he said, for not passing the amendment against slavery. The election made it clear that people wanted to end slavery for all time. Why, then, delay?

Why, indeed?

The Senate had already passed the measure. Now the House joined in. After members came back from their Christmas vacations, they took up the amendment. On the last day of January, 1865, they passed the Thirteenth Amendment, by a big majority.

The Reverend Noah Brooks was in the gallery of the House at the time. Here is what he saw as he watched the fateful event:

> The supreme moment finally arrived. Speaker Colfax's ringing voice demanded of the House, "Shall the Joint Resolution pass?"
>
> The roll-call proceeded, and as the clerk's call went slowly down the list, knots of members gathered around their fellows who were keeping tally. Occasionally, when a member whose

opposition to the amendment had been notable, voted "aye," a clatter of applause, irrepressible and spontaneous, swept through the House.

When the name of John Ganson, a New York Peace Democrat, gave back an echo of "aye," much to the surprise of everybody, there was a great burst of enthusiasm. This marked the safety of the amendment. On the final vote there were one hundred and nineteen in the affirmative, fifty-six in the negative and eight absentees.

When the roll-call was concluded, Speaker Colfax exercised his prerogative and asked the clerk to call his name, whereupon his voice rang out with an "aye."

Then, the record being made up, the Speaker, his voice trembling, said, "On the passage of the Joint Resolution to amend the Constitution of the United States, the ayes have one hundred and nineteen, the noes fifty-six. The constitutional majority of two-thirds having voted in the affirmative, the Joint Resolution has passed."

For a moment there was a pause of utter silence, as if the voices of the dense mass of spectators were choked by strong emotion.

Then there was an explosion, a storm of cheers, the like of which probably no Congress of the United States ever heard before. Strong men embraced each other with tears. The galleries and aisles were bristling with standing, cheering crowds. The air was stirred with a cloud of women's handkerchiefs waving and floating; hands were shaking; men threw their arms about each other's necks, and cheer after cheer and burst after burst followed.

Full ten minutes elapsed before silence returned sufficient to enable Ebon Ingersoll, of Illinois, to move an adjournment "in honor of the sublime and immortal event."

The next day, Lincoln signed the Amendment and sent it to the states, who were sure to ratify it. There was a grand procession, that night, with whites and

Celebration in Washington.

Culver Serv

Negroes walking together. It ended at the White House, with a serenade for the President.

Lincoln went out onto the balcony and said a few words. He had always worked for freedom of the slaves, he reminded them, but his efforts alone were not enough. Now this Amendment settled the matter. "It is the King's cure for all the evils. It winds the whole thing up."

That was it—it wound up the whole thing.

It was the end. It was the end of ownership of man by man. It was the end of a fifty-year struggle by men and women who hated slavery.

Up in Newburyport, Massachusetts, was one of these: the good gray Quaker poet, John Greenleaf Whittier. He wrote his joy and thankfulness in a poem called, "Praise to God":

> It is done.
> Clang of bell and roar of gun.
> Send the tidings up and down.
> How the belfries rock and reel!
> How the great guns, peal on peal,
> Fling the joy from town to town!
>
> Let us kneel:
> God's own voice is in that peal,
> And this spot is holy ground.
> Lord, forgive us! What are we,
> That our eyes this glory see,
> That our ears have heard the sound!

Blotted out!
All within and all about
Shall a fresher life begin;
Freer breathe the universe
As it rolls its heavy curse
On the dead and buried sin!

Ring and swing,
Bells of joy! On morning's wing
Send the song of praise abroad!
With a sound of broken chains
Tell the nations that He reigns
Who alone is Lord and God!

Lincoln, too, came to see the whole war, and the freeing of the slaves, as an unfolding of God's will. This was the theme of his Second Inaugural Address:

One-eighth of the whole population was colored slaves, not distributed generally over the Union, but localized in the southern part of it. These slaves constituted a peculiar and powerful interest. All knew that this interest was somehow the cause of the war. . . .

Neither party expected for the war the magnitude or the duration which it has already attained. Neither anticipated that the *cause* of the conflict might cease with or even before the conflict itself should cease. Each looked for an easier triumph, and a result less fundamental and astounding. Both read the same Bible and pray to the same God, and each invokes His aid against the other.

It may seem strange that any men should dare to ask a just God's assistance in wringing their bread from the sweat of other men's faces, but let us judge not, that we be not judged. The prayers of both could not be answered. That of neither has been answered fully.

The Almighty has His own purposes. "Woe unto the world because of offenses; for it must needs be that offenses come, but woe to that man by whom the offense cometh."

If we shall suppose that American slavery is one of those offenses which, in the providence of God, must needs come, but which, having continued through His appointed time, He now wills to remove, and that He gives to both North and South this terrible war as the woe due to those by whom the offense came, shall we discern therein any departure from those divine attributes which the believers in a living God always ascribe to him?

Fondly do we hope, fervently do we pray, that this mighty scourge of war may speedily pass away. Yet, if God wills that it continue until all the wealth piled by the bondsman's two hundred and fifty years of unrequited toil shall be sunk, and until every drop of blood drawn with the lash shall be paid by another drawn with the sword, as was said three thousand years ago, so still it must be said, "The judgments of the Lord are true and righteous altogether."

*　　*　　*　　*　　*

Now we are almost finished.

The war is almost ended: Richmond is abandoned. Lee is in full retreat, and Grant after him. Just ahead is Appomattox and the final surrender.

Now Lincoln, too, has run his allotted course. Another week, and a madman will silence that noble heart.

There is still one more scene to be played, before the end of this splendid and tragic drama.

When Richmond fell, Lincoln went down to see the city and welcome it back into the Union. Simply, without pomp or show, he walked from the river to the military headquarters. Quickly the word spread to the Negroes of the stricken city. One of the soldiers who saw the scene was moved to describe it:

What a spectacle! I never witnessed such rejoicing in all my life. As the President passed along the street, the colored people waved their handkerchiefs, hats and bonnets, and expressed their gratitude by shouting repeatedly, "Thank God for His goodness. We have seen his salvation!" The white soldiers caught the sound and swelled the numbers, cheering as they marched along.

All could see the President, he was so tall. One woman . . . threw her bonnet in the air, screaming with all her might, "Thank you, Master Lincoln!"

President Lincoln walked in silence, acknowledging the salute of officers and soldiers, and of the citizens, colored and white. It was a man of the people among the people. It was the great deliverer among the delivered.

Lincoln rides through Richmond, April 4, 1865.

No wonder tears
came to his eyes when
he looked on the poor
colored people who
were once slaves, and
heard the blessings
uttered from thankful
hearts.

One ancient Negro
woman asked, "Is that
President Lincoln?"
When told that it really
was, she gazed at him
with clasped hands
and said,

"Glory to God. Give Him the praise for his goodness." And she shouted till her voice failed her.

ACKNOWLEDGMENTS

Grateful acknowledgment is given to the following publishers for permission to use quotations found within this text:

> *The Diary of Gideon Welles,* by Gideon Welles (Houghton Mifflin Company, 1911)
>
> *The Journal of Charlotte Forten,* edited by Ray Billington (The Dryden Press, Inc., 1953)
>
> *Lincoln and the Civil War in the Diaries and Letters of John Hay* (Reprinted in part by permission of Dodd, Mead & Company, Inc., from *Lincoln and the Civil War in the Diaries and Letters of John Hay,* edited by Tyler Dennett. Copyright 1939 by Dodd, Mead & Company, Inc.)